AF661865

SHIVABA

A Gallant Warrior

Dhiraj Navlakhe

Translated by: Aditi Pangarkar Puranik

Price: 100/-

VARADA PRAKASHAN PVT. LTD.
Varada, Senapati Bapat Road, 397/1, Vetalbaba Chowk, Pune-411016
Tel.: 020-25655654, Mob. 9970169302
Email: varadaprakashan@gmail.com
Website: www.varadabooks.com

Content

Shivaba - A Gallant Warrior

Printers and Publishers:
Varada Prakashan Pvt. Ltd

Printing Place:
Trinity Academy for Corporate Training, Pune

© Gaurav Gaur (August 2023)

Cover Design: Dhiraj Navlakhe

First Edition: September 2023

ISBN: 978-81-19363-18-6

1.

BIRTH OF A WARRIOR "SHIVAJI MAHARAJ"

यदा यदा ही धर्मस्य ग्लानिर्भवति भारत ।

अभ्युत्थानमधर्मस्य तदात्मानम सृज्याहम ॥

परित्राणाय साधूनां विनाशाय च दुष्कृताम ।

धर्म संस्थापनार्थाय संभवामि युगे युगे ॥

Friends, Lord Krishna from Bhagvad Gita tells us that whenever the natural law and conscience (dharma) will be in peril, to salvage it, to guard the seers and saints, to destroy the wicked and restore the dharma the moral order, Lord Krishna will reincarnate himself on earth. The birth of Shivaji Maharaj, endorses this. The reign of the Mughals tortured and exploited the common man on Marathi soil. The wars and battles fought by

Adilshah and Nizamshah oppressed the poor people. The Adilshahi and Nizamshahi regimes plundered the towns and villages. The levy of unjust taxes and atrocities committed by Mughal army on women and children further deteriorated the situation. The onslaught of droughts and famines added to the miseries. The people were dying of hunger. The devil of anarchy possesed the society and the dharma had gone into deep slumber. It was the golden day of 19.2.1630. The entire Shivneri fort was engrossed. Dadoji Konddev, the administrator of Shahji's jagir was anxiously moving around the palace. The sentiment of anxiety and excitement both co-existed everywhere. What was bothering the people? Everyone was anxiously waiting to hear the "good news". Jijabai had gone into labour! Dadoji Konddev was nervous and prayed Goddess Shivaai seeking blessings for the well-being of baby and mother.

Just a moment later there was a creaking noise and the door of the bedroom opened. The midwife with a pleasant smile announced the birth of a baby boy... Everybody rejoiced with happiness. Dadoji Konddev

was the happiest. Instantly, he took off the pearl necklace he was wearing and handed it to the midwife as a token of appreciation. Dadoji Konddev was overjoyed and desperate to reveal Shahji the news that a son was born to him. There was considerable upheaval at that time in Maharashtra. The Mughal emperor 'Shahjahan' was approaching Deccan with his huge army from north. Adilshah also had deployed his army at that time at Pune. The army had completely destroyed the city. During that time Shahaji maharaj was a Commander (Sardar) under Nijamshah. So Shahaji maharaj asked his wife Jijabai to move to Shivneri fort for safety. And he went to Khandesh to fight with Daryakhan. Shahaji maharaj was a diligent and brave Commander. Initially Raja Shahaji was Commander under Nijamshah and was very popular. However he was not in accord with Minister of Nijamshah Malik Amber. So had to switch side with Adilshah of Vijapur. Adilshah conferred the title 'Commander in chief ' (Sarlashkar) on him. After the death of 'Malik Amber' , the grip of Nijamshahi weakened, and circumstances prompted Nijamshah's mother to reinstate Raja Shahji into the service of Nijamshah. Raja Shahji now served Nijamshah. Dadoji Kondadev became conscious of his duty, and made a gesture to the guard on the fort. He immediately ignited the cannon with flaming torch. And there was a loud 'boom' which was indicating the birth of a baby boy. The Shivneri Fort resonated with happiness and celebration. A few days later Jijabai announced the naming ceremony of her baby. All women thronged the fort suggesting names for the baby. However, there was a spark in Jijabai's eyes and she was firm and determined. Jijabai belived that the baby was born with the blessings of Shivai Devi and she named her baby 'Shivaji'.

2.

CHILDHOOD

"Shivaba, dear Shivaba, don't run dear" Jijabai ran after the baby steps. Shivaba was very swift, it was nearly impossible for Jijabai to get hold of him at times when Shivaba hid in some nook, tracing him was an arduous act. Jijau was happy with the fact that Shivaba was a clever and wise child.

Running after Shivaba was almost a daily affair for Jijabai. She was a doting mother. During the evenings Jijai made Shivaba sit with her and recite prayers. It was instrumental in shaping Shivaba's character. She made him pay respect to all the elderly present in the house. These rituals had layed foundation of a humble and cultured Shivaji. Jijau had a lion's share in positively moulding Shivaba's character. The little Shivaba sat on Jijau's lap, and very keenly listened the stories of brave Lord Ram, powerful Hanuman and of the ideal brothers Laxman and Bharat. She also narrated stories of Lord Krishna who destroyed the devils, of the uprighteous conduct of Pandavas and of the determined and focused Ekalavya.

Shivaba listened these stories with great awe and attention. He drew great inspiration from them. As a result, his intellect was sharpened and he learned his first lessons of warfare.

Shivaba was growing up. Now he started playing with children of the Mavlas on Shivneri fort. All of them together played a unique game called 'the King and his subjects.' On one occasion Shivaba had assumed the role of a king and his fellow Mavla friends the ministers. Shivaba in a commanding and royal voice addressed the chief minister, "Pradhanji, let's commence today's proceedings!" The chief minister said, "My Lord, today there is a legal matter to be adjudicated. An individual

from the kingdom has abused one woman. She is in tears. Shivaba ordered his fellow friends to produce the man before him. They humbly produced one of their fellow Mavlas as 'the man' before Shivaba and said, "Your Lordship, this is the person who has abused the woman."

Shivaba observed that Mavla, and pondered for a moment. Jijau had been watching this spectacle from window and was eager to see Shivaba's future course of action.

Shivaba thoughtfully said, "Any woman be it from our kingdom or other kingdom, we will never tolerate the injustice caused to her. Mutilate off the hands and legs of this individual with which he tortured the woman. Protecting our mothers and sisters is our fundamental duty and responsibility."

Jijau was very happy. She felt proud of the fact that Shivaba had great respect towards women. The judicious sence that Shivaba possessed was later reflected through his conduct when he became the king.

Shivaba ws affectionate towards everyone since childhood. He never discriminated between rich and poor, instead played happily with the children of hardworking Mavlas and the children of the farmers. He visited their homes and ate chutney-bhakri with them. He drank water from their homes and played with these children treating them as equals.

The attributes of justice, equally, fraternity were imbued in himsince childhood.

Shahaji raje to save Nijamshahi, fought with the Mughals and Adilshah with full might. However, the huge armies of Mughal and Adilshah defeated him. Ultimately he surrendered the Mughals. The Mughals and Adilshah apportioned the Nijamshahi amongst them and Shahaji raje started serving Adilshah as Jahgirdaar. Adilshah sent Shahaji raje to Karnataka, so Shahaji raje, alongwith Shivaba and Jijabai moved to Karnataka. As Shivaba grew, he started getting lessons of polity and armoury. Adilshah once again sent Shahaji raje on a mission and so Shahaji raje asked Jijabai and Shivaba to shift to Pune.

When Shivaba was ten years old, he entered into wedlock with Saibai of Nimbalkars from Phaltan.

As Shivaba entered the twelfth year, Jijabai made arrangements for his higher education. To train Shivaji in warfare and politics, she entrusted Dadoji Konddev the responsibility of training him. Dadoji Konddev gave lessons to him in horse-riding, sword and spear handling and archery. He made Shivaba study the ancient Indian texts of the Shruti, Puran, Vedas, Ramayan and Mahabharat. By now Shivaba had become proficient. He had developed a sharp intellect and the ingrained knowledge gave him foresight. The education made him mature and positively altered his thinking patterns. Shivaba became more determined and resolved. He had now entered the youth.

3.

THE HERALD OF SWARAJYA

Shivaba had now entered into fifteenth year, fair complexion, robust body, black prominent eyes, he looked radiant and handsome. Shivaba alongwith his friends on horse back, started exploring the Sahyadri mountains and settlement at the foothills. The huge mountains, the wild fragrances, the cascades and the melodious sonore of the flowing rives beckoned him.

Shivaba alongwith his friends easily ascended the steep rocks. It had become his adventure and passion. Shivaba watched rhe poor, oppressed and toiling masses and he was moved. Shivaba had a soft corner towards them. He desperately wanted to help them.

Once, early morning Shivaba alongwith his friends left for exploring the hills. It was monsoon, there were water droplets on the emerald green leaves which shimmered when the early morning sunbeams danced on them. The mountains were carpeted all green. The humming of the birds pleased the ears. All of them were happy and they were wandering. They approached a village. It was the village bazaar and there were huge crowds of people. Shivaba's gaze fell on Mughal soldiers who were forcibly trying to recover tax from a vendor. Shivaba and his friends witnessed the scene. All of them became serious and silent.

The Mughal army recovered the tax and left away. The very moment, Shivaba swiftly mounted on his horse and rode away speedily. The friends were perplexed and they followed Shivaba. Amidst the forests and mountains Shivaba's horse galloped swiftly and speedily.

Suddenly , Shivaba stopped on the bank of a river. He was now staring at a waterfall intensely. His chest was heaving up and down, his breath became fast, his face was red with rage and there was fire in his eyes. The friends noticed him finally and amongst them, Netaji asked him anxiously with utmost concern, " Shivaba, what is the matter? What is bothering you? Let me know your concern, I am like a friend."

Shivaba's chain of thoughts was interrupted and he said, "I am not understanding. My mind is agonized, how can I tolerate such grave injustice in front of my eyes?"

Netaji said, "Shivaba, tell me your intention!"

Shivaba mounted on his horse and gesticulated Netaji to follow him. Everybody else followed Shivaba. They arrived at the Raireshwar Temple. Shivaba threw one glance on everyone and said, "Dear friends, these mountains, rivers, this beautifully blossomed earth that we are perceiving is not free and is being trampled under the feet of Mughals. All of us are just mute spectators. We are responsible for the injustice caused to our people and our land. We are failing to uphold our Dharma! Is it not sinful to witness the atrocities committed on our fellow brothers and sisters without doing anything."

Immediately Netaji asked, “Shivaba, do you have any plans?”

Shivaba became grave and taking a deep breath said, “I want to establish our own kingdom (self-role), our Swarajya! I wish to free our land from the bondage of Mughals and Adilshahi. Would you like to help me in this endeavor?”

Everybody looked at each other and unanimously said in one voice, “Yes Shivaba, we are with you!”

Shivaba said, “So then dear friends, let us take a pledge.” They raised their hands and avowed. “ We are ready to sacrifice our lives to achieve Swarajya!”

Netaji, in great admiration looked towards Shivaba. He felt proud. All of them joined their hands in prayer in front of Lord Mahadev and in a raised voice in unison said, “ Har Har Mahadev!” The entire ambience resonatedwith the pious and divine acclimation of Lord Mahadev. Every Mavla was inspired and moved. “ Our own Kingdom!” The idea of this concept made them ecstatic. They achieved a new vision and direction.

Shivaba seeked blessings from Jijau and the foudation for Swarajya was layed.

4.

RAPID STRIDES TOWARDS SWARAJYA

After having sworn, at Raireshwar Temple, Shivaba and all Mavlas starting working together towards their goal. However, establishing Swarajya was an arduous task. The state of Maharashtra was at the same time ruled by the Badshah of Delhi, Adilshah of Vijapur, Portugese of Goa and Siddis of Janjira. They had apportioned the entire Maharashtra amongst them. Shivaba with his handful Mavlas had to defeat the massive army of all the rulers. Shivaba's resolve and confidence was always stronger than the enemy's power. Shivaba passionately worked towards Swarajya. He critically studied the adjoining area, the forts located in these areas. The

Vatandars and Deshmukhs were always engaged in duel amongst themselves which was a reason of disharmony. Shivaba explained the significance of Swarajya to them. There were some who willingly consented and joined Shivaji in this venture. However, there were others who wreaked havoc and had to be skillfully inducted. He brought everybody together and convinced them about their true strength which was unity.

Once, Shivaba was looking out of window and contemplating on something. At that moment Tanaji Malusare, a brave Mavla stepped in. He was able to read the anxiety on Shivaba's face and said, "My Lord, everything is going on well, yet you seem to be concerned? You are striving for the well being of our people."

Shivaba turned towards him and said," This is not enough for Swarajya. We need to conquer the forts. "Again he looked out of the window and pointed towards the Torna fort. "Watch the Torna fort. It is ideally located and is robust. We can keep a watch on

Shivrai now commenced the administration of fort. He appointed the Killedars, head guard of the fort, Brahmins and other officers. Everyone worked promptly keeping in mind the ideals of Swarajya.

The fort was in need of repairs. The task commenced and the Mavlas discovered four earthen pots of gold coins. They immediately handed it over to Shivrai. The glittering gold failed to rouse any lust in them. Shivrai was impressed by their honesty and fidelity the gold was used to purchase cannon-balls, swords and spears and shields. They took possession of nearby fort ,repaired and reconstructed it naming it 'Raigad'.

Thereafter successively, Shivrai conquered the forts of Kondhana, Purandar and Rohida. The winds of Swarajya were flowing in all directions scattering the flowers of victory.

all the surrounding adjoining areas from there. We must conquer this fort."

With protruding chest Tanaji was quick to reply," Lordship, we are awaiting your command. Adilshah is not so attentive towards it and the fort is not properly guarded. Just let us know when to ascend!"

Shivaji felt relieved and admired this statement of Tanaji. Striking an ideal timing, Shivrai grouped the Mavlas and all of them arrived at the foothills of the Torna fort. The spirit of Swarajya had possessed the young Mavlas. All of them were eager and enthusiastic since it was their first attempt.

"My lionhearted companions, lets ascend the fort, free it from the clutches of Mughals and seize it! Aai Bhavani's blessings are with us!" These words roused the spirit in the Mavlas and they swiftly ascended the fort. They seized the prominent areas and the unanticipated attack terrorized the guards. They conquered the fort and Hindu Swarajya flag was unfurled.

5.

SAFEGUARDING SWARAJYA FROM HOSTILE ENEMIES

The noble court had commenced its daily business. At that time one of the Mavlas entered the hall and delivered an important message. " Your Lordship, there is a letter from Chandrarao More of Javli."

Adilshah had conferred 'Jahgirdari' on Chandrarao More of Javal region commencing from Raigad and ending at the Koyna valley. Amongst them Daulatrao More had died and there was a feud amongst his sons to claim "Jahgirdari'. During that period, Shivrai had helped one of the brothers, Yashwantrao More to secure

the ‘Jahgirdari’. In turn he had consented to help Shivrai to attain Swarajya.

The moment he ascended the throne, he refused to help Shivrai. Shivrai had sent him a letter ,”Yashwantrao, please don’t commit the mistake of assuming yourself to be the King. I am the King, come with me to attain Swarajya.”

Yashwantrao More had sent a letter as a reply forthwith. One of the Mavlas started reading a letter,” Shivaj, you assert yourself to be a King, however, let me know the entity who conferred the title of nobility on you. Adilshah has bestowed the title of King on me, and so don’t you dare to commit the mistake of interfering!’

Shivrai made final attempt to give an understanding to Yashwantrao More. Yashwantrao refused the amicable proposal and so Shivaji decided to teach him a lesson.

Shivrai entered upon Javal region and there was a combat between Shivrai and Yashwantrao More, which finally culminated in defeat of Yashwantrao. Thereafter, More, alongwith his family, went to Rairi. Shivaji chased him there and ultimately he surrendered. The fort was conquered by Shivaji and renamed it as 'Raigad'.

In a similar fashion, Khandoji and Baji Ghorpade, under Adilshah, conspired agaist Shivaji. However,their army failed to withstand the powerful Mavlas. Bajaji Naik Nimbalkar,in a clandestine manner, joined hands with Adilshahand plotted against Shivaji. Shivrai launched an attack on Phaltan and Bajaji Naik was defeated.

Shivrai in such manner, castigated many 'Jahgirdars' who were ready to be enslaved under Adilshah for selfish motives.

Shivrai always rebelled against injustice, even when the person causing injustice were his relatives or near and dear ones. Shivaba spared nobody, whosoever caused impediment in attaining Swarajya was dealt with severely

6.

AFZHALKHAN

Adilshah of Vijapur was aware of the expanding kingdom and popularity of Shivaji Maharaj. That day in the court of Adilshah, many famous and powerful soldiers were present. Everyone's mind was haunted with the same difficulty and that was getting rid of Shivaji Maharaj. They knew that killing Shivaji Maharaj was nearly impossible All the courtiers were pondering. Adilshah remained silent, however his mind was stormed with anger.One of the Begum was enraged and screamed."How is it that this silly naïve Shivaji is offending us"?We are all mute spectators to Shivaji grabbing our Sultanate. She glanced the soldiers and said "Is there not a single soldier amongst us who can kill Shivaji"?. Everyone was silent. Just then one of the soldier's rose and advanced. He was well-built, tall and powerful. They called him Afzhalkhan. Afzhalkhan said "I will bring Shivaji here alive and if that is not possible, present his decapitated head to you"! He mockingly said" Shivaji is nothing for me and left the hall.

Afzhalkhan well armed alongwith his huge army left for his mission. He was haughty and had false belief that he could kill Shivaji.

Shivaba was very well aware of the intentions of Afzhalkhan. He had already gathered information about his large armyand weaponry. However, Shivaji was clever and wise enough to decipher that it would be folly to fight Afzhalkhan on the battlefield and devised a plan.

Shivarai arrived on Pratapgad and Afzhalkhan understood this. The topography of Pratapgad was unsuitable to enable the huge army to ascend it. Afzhalkhan was furious. He tried his best to bring Shivaji at the foothills. When nothing worked, he feigned good conduct. He sent a letter to Shivaji saying, "Shivaji, forgive me dear. You are like my son. Come and meet me."

Instantly Shivaji understood his treachery and he planned something. He sent a letter to Afzhalkhan saying, "Khansaheb, I misunderstood your intentions, thereby offending you. I am eager to meet you, yet I am afraid of you so please come and meet me."

Afzhalkhan was fooled by the correspondence and became indolent. Shivrai informed him the place, date and timing of the meeting. The place was at foothills of Pratapgad. There Shivrai errected one awning.

On the decided day, Afzhalkhan arrived at the awning. Shivrai wanted to ascertain his moves, so he left late. He was accompanied by Jivaji Mahala and ten bodyguards. Just before leaving he wore tiger claw weapons metal belt weapon to his waist. He prayed before Bhavanidevi and approached and finally arrived at the gate of awning. He saw Afzhalkhan seated in, reclined fashionand next to him was a soldier named

Sayyad Banda. Shivrai asked him to leave awning and wait ouside.

Shivrai entered the awning and Instantly Afzhalkhan rose and said, “Come dear Shivaji, let me embrace you.”

Jivaji Mahala was standing at the gate of awning. Afzhalkhan embraced Shivrai tightening his grip and plunged the dagger into his abdomen. However, since Shivaji wore an armour, it didn’t harm him. Very skillfully, Shivrai plunged the sharp tiger claws in Afzhalkhan’s stomach and with the other hand sruck a narrow sharp blade. Afzhalkhan smeared with blood, collapsed on the ground. Sayyad Banda was about to attack Shivrai when Jivaji Mahala intervened and alarmed Shivaji. Instantly he removed the sword fastened to his waist, and struck a blow on Sayyad Banda on his arm, chopping off his hand. He immediately chopped off his head.

Shivrai with immense admiration glanced Jivaji. His chest swelled with pride. “My dear friend, you saved me. Jiva saved Shiva.” Both of them were overjoyed and their eyes were moist. They reached the Pratapgad and cannons of victory were fired. There was jubilation and celebration everywhere.

7.

GHODKHIND BECOMES PAWANKHIND

The monsoon had commenced. It was raining heavily. Shivaji maharaj was at Panhalgad. A barber was cutting his hair. Shivaji Maharaj was tensed. He was engrossed in thinking. Reading his face, the barber asked him, “Maharaj, what is troubling you so much?” Shivrai was (affable) to every single person.

Shivrai came out of labyrinth of thoughts and said, “The death of Afzhalkahn has enraged the Badshah of Vijapur. As you are aware that he has summonned Siddi Johar and Fazalkhan, Afzhalkhan’s son to incarcerate me.”

"Very true your Lordship! It is almost three months and yet we are under siege imposed by them. The food stock is not enough to sustain us for a long period. It would be difficult for us to stay here. As compared to their enormous army, our Mavlas are few. It is not ideal to battle with their army."

The barber immediately asked Shivaji Maharaj if he could be of any help.

Something struck Shivaji's mind. "Your name is also Shivaji, right?"

"Yes, your lordship"

Shivrai asked him, "Would you like to work for Swarajya?"

"I would sacrifice my life, your Lordship!"

Shivrai gave him an affectionate look and gave a pat on his back. Subsequently, Shivrai alongwith advocate Gangadhar, Bajiprabhu Deshpande and others devised a plan. Accordingly, the barber was made to sit in one sedan whereas Shivaji Maharaj sat in the other.

The barber's sedan commenced from the regular route whereas, the sedan of Shivaji Maharaj followed a different route.

The news that Shivaji is escaping from a sedan fell on the ears of the army of Siddi Johar. They unknowingly arrested the barber's sedan and rejoiced assuming he was Shivaji.

Taking advantage of their ignorance, Shivaji Maharaj left towards Vishalgad. Siddi Johar after some time realized that the arrested was not Shivaji, but his barber and instantly he sent his soldiers after Shivaji.

Shivrai had reached Ghodkhind. The fact that the army was after him had already reached him. Shivarai said to Bajiprabhu, "Vishalgad is quite far! The army is close to us. How can we reach Vishalgad? Wouldn't it be ideal if we fight them here itself!"

Bajiprabhu was quick to reply, "Dear Shivaba, this is the right moment of proving my loyalty. I will stay back with Mavlas and fight the army. You move ahead to Vishalgad with few Mavlas and when you reach there, fire a cannon. Till then I will stay here!"

With immense admiration, Shivaji Maharaj embraced Bajiprabhu and said, "Goddess Bhavani's blessings are with you!" Bajiprabhu alongwith other Mavlas amassed boulders, large branches of trees and logs of wood. The first division of army of enemy approached Ghodkhind. Instantly, all Mavlas started pelting stones, branches and logs of wood at them. They were gravely injured and finally died. The remaining soldiers were killed by Bajiprabhu. The next division of army arrived and again mavlas attacked them with stones and boulders. Amidst the fight, Bajiprabhu was raising the spirits of mavlas. "Bravo, my dear friends, kill each one of them!". Bajiprabhu was possesed with anger and he mercilessly killed the enemy soldiers. Suddenly, one of the enemy soldier's attacked him from behind. As a result, Bajipraphu was wounded. He was in deep agony yet continued the fight. The second division of army was also defeated. Now, the third division of army arrived. Shivray was yet to reach the fort. But as promised,

Bajiprabhu fought till his last breath. How could he give up without fulfilling his promise?. He was smeared with blood yet he fought. He was still boosting the mavlas" My dear friends, fight with might!.Let every drop of your blood be put to use to achieve swarajya. Shivray uptill now had reached the foothills of Vishalgad.The army of the enemy stationed there tried to arrest Shivaji maharaj however Shivarai gave them a tough fight and they were defeated. Bajiprabhu was battling death just to hear the sound of canon. Suddenly, Bajiprabhu heard the booming sound, he was now relieved, and closed his eyes forever. It was this strong support of warriors like Bajiprabhu which helped Shivaji maharaj accomplish swarajya.

8.

SHAISTAKHAN'S DEFEAT

Year after year passed yet Shaistekhan, the maternal uncle of Aurangzeb was not ready to move out of Lal Mahal. Shivaji had now started conquering the empires of the Mughals in North India which led to growing discontent amongst the rulers. Aurangzeb was extremely anxious and so he sent Shaistakhan, (maternal uncle) with huge army, elephants, horses and canons to Pune. Shaistekhan sabotaged many villages in Maharashtra, he captured the Purandar fort and Chakan fort and now had shifted his base to Lal Mahal in Pune. Shaistekhan sent his troops to nearby villages and caused immense trouble and destruction. Shivaji Maharaj resolved to get rid of this menace and so, alongwith his faithful and loyal Mavlas devised a plan.

It was late night. A wedding procession was going to pass along Lal Mahal. Shivai, alongwith his Mavlas, joined the procession. The procession arrived infront of Lal Mahal. The loud noise of the procession distracted the guards stationed on Lal Mahal. Taking advantage of this situation, Shivarai and the Mavlas entered the Lal Mahal stealthily. There was not sufficient light. The torch flame were off. The guards were sleepy and yawning. The Mavlas skillfully sealed their mouths and tied their hands and legs. Now Shivrai and the Mavlas moved towards the kichen hall. This facilitated easy entry inside the Mahal. Shivai was aware of every nook and corner of Lal Mahal. All of them entered the kichen hall and killed the royal cooks. Some of the Mavlas entered the drum house and asked the drum players to play Nagadas and Dholaks. Amidst the chaotic pandemonium, the guards were confused and started running helter-skelter.

In the meantime, someone tried to assault Shivaji, however Shivaji killed that person who was the son of Shaistakhan. Shivaji entered into Shaistakhan's bedroom. Shaistekhan instantly woke up due to the noise and chaos. Shivaji immediately attacked Shaistakhan with sword, however Shaistekhan threw a cushion and it hit the cushion. Shaistekhan swiftly rose and started running away. Shivaji chased him, Shaistekhan now entered the Harem and hid himself behind a curtain.

Shivai just glanced and he spotted Shaistekhan's hand. He ran towards him. Shaistakhan now approached a window and tried to jump off. However, before he could escape, Shivaji attacked him with sword. The blow struck Shaistekhan's hand and his fingers. Shaistekhan was smeared with blood and in the injured state ran away.

Shivai and the Mavlas in raised voice started shouting, " Look! Shivaji comes!" The noise further created noise and confusion amidst the guards, and in the meantime Shivai and the Mavlas left the Lal Mahal. Shaistekhan was terrorized by the incident and alongwith his guards fled away.

The news fell on Aurangzeb's ears, and he was mad with rage. All his efforts had been wasted. Shivaji had defeated such a huge army with a handful of Mavlas in no time. Aurangzeb understood the valour, bravery and prowess of Shivaji Maharaj.

9.

HEADING TOWARDS SURAT

Shaistekhan within three days of defeat had fled away..! The news was revealed to Shivaji Maharaj by one of his spy. The entire Rajgad shone with happiness.

Shaistekhan during his stay of three years, had destabilized Swarajya.

How to compensate the loss was a haunting question for Shivaji Maharaj. To re-establish the Swarajya, he needed money. At the same time, establishing a navy on the west coast was equally essential to safeguard it. Shivaji Maharaj realized that Surat which was situated at the west coast, was the only solution.

Surat was a trading hub during role of Aurangzeb, a wealthy and prosperous city. It was the richest port on west coast of India. At Surat, trade worth in crores took place. The English, Dutch, Portuguese, Persians, Africans, Chinese and other foreigners traded at Surat. The diamonds, pearls, gold, spices and condiments, silk, perfumes and utensils were major chunk of this trade. It was a largest market thronged with people and merchants.

Shivaji Maharaj was determined to recover the compensation for losses cused to Swarajya. Shivaji Maharaj instantly sent one of his spies Bahirji Naik on the mission of fetching details about Surat. He came back with accurate details. He disguised himself in multiple fashions moving from square to square, in the markets and the streets. All the whereabouts and minutest details were with him now.

Shivaji Maharaj set out for Surat mission himself. On 6th December 1663, Shivrai left for Surat which was about 270 miles from Rajgad.

Shivaji Maharaj journeyed during the nights and during day time, rested in the jungles so that nobody knew about his presence. Finally, he reached Surat. The city was engrossed in its daily affairs. All the merchants, rich people were busy in trading. As Shivaji entered into the city with his brigade, everyone started shouting, " Look Shivaji is here! Shivaji has come!" Everywhere people were running helter-skelter and the city was drowned in chaos and confusion. The merchants, the elites and the traders were running away.

The governor of Surat was Inayatkhan. Shivaji Maharaj had written a letter demanding ransom and had threatened him to meet personally. He had also put a condition that in case he fails to observe this, the entire Surat will be looted. Inayatkhan denied the proposal and didn't even come out of his fort. Seeing nobody is taking cognizance Shivrai commanded the Mavlas to enter the commercial area. The Mavlas arrived, breaking the door and gained forceful entery in the palacious houses of the rich traders and merchants. They amassed the precious jewelry, diamonds and pearls from their houses, breaking their lockers.

Adjacent to Inayatkhan's fort, there was a customs booth. The Mavlas jumped into the customs booth from tower of the fortand emptied the entire customs booth. The Mavlas were looting everywhere gathering large sums of money, treasury in purses and bags and placing them infront of Maharaj. However, they had strict instructions from Shivaji Maharaj to not even touch children, women, fakirs, the poor people and the Dargahs.

The intention of Shivaji Maharaj was very honest and transparent and that was to take possession of the illegal wealth belonging to Aurangzeb.

The Mavlas were looting for two consecutive days and nights. They had now bullock carts filled with the loot money. On the third day, one of the spies of Shivaji Maharaj announced that Aurangzeb's chief Mahabat Khan was going to arrive with huge army. Immediately

taking the loot alongwith them, they moved out of the city.

Shivaji Maharaj never wished to loot Surat for his own selfish gains but, for establishing Swarajya. The loot was compensation for the large sums of money plundered by Aurangzeb for three consecutive years. Moreover, he had legally intimated the governer about the same. Yet, the governor didn't pay heed to it. He failed to understand the strength of Shivaji Maharaj and considered his silence as his weakness and so Maharaj was left with no other alternative but to loot the city.

10.

TREATY OF PURANDAR

The corpse of Murarbaji Deshpande was lying and witnessing the sight, an agonized Shivaji Maharaj was in tears. The life of brave courageous warrior had come to an end. Shivaji was upset and looking at Jijau he asked, "Ausaheb, we have lost the valuable jem in process of attaining Swarajya. Is this right?"

Jijau in an assuring tone said to him, "Shivaba, I can comprehend the state of your mind. You killed the most powerful soldiers of Aurangzeb, you got rid of Shaistekhan and now you looted the richest trading city of Surat, belonging to Mughal. So, Aurangzeb has sought vengeance agaist this."

Shivrai very angrily said, " Ausaheb, we looted Surat to teach a lesson to Aurangzeb who had been responsible for the damage caused to our people."

"Dear Shivaba, we shouldn't forget that Aurangzeb being a despotic in order to pamper his ego, can go to any extent. And that is why he has sent Mirza Raje Jaisingh and Dilerkhan to Maharashtra."

"Indeed Ausaheb, seiged Purandar with his troops and our brave warrior Murarbaji Deshpande while guarding a fort was killed. Our Mavlas are still fighting against Dilerkhan but I wonder how will they sustain 20000 soldiers of Dilerkhan when they are only 2000 in number. Our every Mavla is brave and courageous and will continue to be so till the end. However, if all our Mavlas continue to get engulfed in the fire of death, how will we achieve Swarajya? I don't see any ray of hope." Shivaji said.

Jijau read Shivaba's face and said, "Shivaba, don't be so upset. Aai Bhavani's blessings are with us. At

times, it is advisable to take a small retreat to reach the zenith."

Shivaji was finally convinced. He went to meet Mirza Raje Jaisingh who was a trusted and brave commander of Aurangzeb. Aurangzeb had sent him on the mission to trick Shivaji and make him vulnerable.

However, Shivaji was not to be easily defeated. He was a diplomatic too. Shivaji entered into a treaty with Jaysingh where he was promised 23 forts, the area generating revenue of 4 lack Hons and a meeting with Aurangzeb at Agra.

Aurangzeb was now under the impression that Shivaji had softened,and cowed, howeverr he had not understood the fact that this was Shivaji Maharaj's next move.

11.

EMPEROR'S MITHAI

"Dear father, how will we return to Shivneri?" a little Sambhaji asked his father. The dark grey clouds of fear were gathering in his eyes. Shivrai hugged Sambhaji and caressed his hands over Sambhaji's face.

Shivaji said, " My dear child, my people call me a tiger, if I be the tiger, then you should be tiger's cub. You should be brave and courageous! Shivaji narrated his ordeal when he had gone to meet Aurangzeb. "We arrived here at Agra to meet Aurangzeb. He insulted me by asking me to stand in the last row and has detained both of us. As you grow you will encounter such challenges, during these times you will be required to

my child! You tricked the emperor!" Sambhaji quickly replied, "I just gave him sweets."

12.

SINHAGAD

A considerable time had passed since arrival of Shivaji maharaj from Agra. The major portion of the kingdom had been lost by way of treaties. Shivaji maharaj was discussing this vital issue with Jijaaau.

Jijaau said, "Shivaba, twenty three forts are under possesion of the Mughals and amongst them Kondhana being a powerful fort is of immense value. Shivaji said, "I agree with you and I am of the same opinion. Shivaji maharaj's discussion with Jijaau was interrupted by one of the mavla. He said, "Maharaj when we have a braveheart like Tanaji Malusare with us, why do you take pains to go on the battlefield"? Tanaji was a diligent

and loyal mavla. Shivaji maharaj asked Tanaji "What makes you come here when your son Rayba is gettting married, your family needs you the most". Tanaji replied "Yes your lordship, in fact I had come with Shelar mama to give you the invitation and I heard your conversation with Jijaau."

"When is Rayba's marriage?" asked Shivaji maharaj. Tanaji quickly pulled out the sword fastened to his waist and said, " Let me first get back Kondhana! Only when I get back Kondhana fort, Rayba will get married!" said Tanaji with iron resolve. Shivaji maharaj tried convincing him yet he was firm on his decision. He was a devout, courageous fighter. He had already made up his mind.

Tanaji alongwith his brother Suryaji led a battalion of eight hundread mavlas to the foothills of Kondhana. It was night, pitch dark and the sound of crickets was prominent. The task of ascending the fort was arduous . The fort was tall. However the mavlas were expert and clever. They carried with them a wild monitored lizard named Yashwanti. They tied a rope around Yashwanti which they mounted on the fort and with the aid of it, all the Mavlas ascended the fort. They jumped inside the fort.

A rajput named Udaybhan was in possession of fort. He came to know about presence of Mavlas and immediately commanded his soldiers. The soldiers and Mavlas now engaged in a fierce battle. The Mavlas attacked them with swords and their swords were smeared with the blood of enemy.

Udaybhan entered the battlefield. He was a gallant. Udaybhan and Tanaji came in face to face. Both were fighting with might. Tanaji like a famished lion was attacking his pray. Amidst the fight Udaybhan's sword pierced Tanaji's shield and it broke. Instantly Tanaji made is left hand his shield and endured all wounds Tanaji's hand was smeared with blood; the pains were unbearable and his head became numb. Taking advantage of Tanaji's condition Udaybhan stabbed his sword in Tanaji's abdomen. Tanaji Instantly struck the sword on Udaybhan's neck. Udaybhan died and even Tanaji collapsed.

The Mavlas broke open the door of the fort. Suryaji alongwith five hundred Mavlas came inside. They started fighting, however they noticed that Tanaji had died. They started escaping. Suryaji quickly noticed and with enraged raised voice rebuked them. "Our prime lionis dead and you are running away like rats? Have you forgotten that you are Shivaji Maharaj's Mavlas? How can you be so coward? What will your children and wives think of you? How will you face Shivaji Maharaj? Come back and fight with might!"

The spirit of Mavlas was roused with the inspiring word of Suryaji, and with full might they destroyed the army of Udaybhan. The Mavlas had won the fort.

Shivaji heard the news. He was proud of his Mavlas, yet deeply agonized with the death of Tanaji. With tears in eyes he said, "I won the fort but lost my lion!"

Thereafter Shivaji Maharaj named Kondhana fort as 'Sinhagad', the fort of lion.

13.

CORONATION

A great scholar and one of the well wishers of Shivaji Maharaj from Kashi, named Gagabhatt paid visit to him.He was discussing with Shivaji Maharaj and Jijamata. Gagabhatt said, "Raje, you have won back entire your kingdom. Even the emperor of Vijapur has asserted to the fact. Now it is the time that the whole world understands that you are a king for which your coronation is necessary."

Jijamata said, "Shivaba, with exemplary courage, facing all odds you have established Swarajya. This has been my dream since long time. We all were aspiring for establishment of Swarajya and its King."

Shivaji Maharaj agreed with Jijamata and Gagabhatt. He consented for coronation and started preparations. Shivai chose Raigad as capital since it was a robust and ideal fort. It was desirable to handle the daily affairs from there.

Thereafter, a golden throne studded with different gems was crafted. A golden parasol was erected on it. All the essential material for coronation was fetched. All the Brahmins and Kings from different Kingdoms were invited.

It was 6 June 1674, the day of coronation. Everybody was busy with preparations on the fort Raigad. All the doors and windows were adorned with lovely decorations of flowers, saffron colour flags were planted everywhere. The melodious notes of musical instruments were resonating on entire Raigad. The chanting of holy mantras added to the piety. Everyone was happy and enthusiastic. Gradually, guests arrived at the fort. More than fifty thousand people had gathered to witness this unique celebration.

The most precious moment arrived. Shivaji Maharaj was made to sit a golden elevated platform. The purohits were pouring ghee, curd and honey on Maharaj for Abhishek and the coronation commenced. Gagabhatt poured water of seven holy rivers once again for Abhishek. They wiped his body with muslin. Jijamata was witnessing this ceremony and her heart was filled with joy and there were tears in her eyes.

Thereafter, Shivaji Maharaj donned a royal robe and he was adorned with pearl necklace. Then Gagabhatt placed the crown on his head and handed him the ceremonial sword and said, "Chhatrapati Shivaji Maharaj ki jay!"

Everyone praised Shivaji Maharaj. The sacrifice made by warriors like Tanaji, Bajiprabhu was rewarded. The pledge taken at Raireshwar Temple was fulfilled.

14.

THE END

It had been eleven days since the coronation. Shivaji Maharaj was having discussions with ministers of his advisory committee. At that moment one of the Mavlas precipitated towards them. He appeared terrified and panicky. When Maharaj asked him what had happened he was speechless. He broke into tears and cried loudly and said, “Maharaj, Ma saheb has left us”.

It was a severe blow to Shivaji Maharaj. It was as if his pillar of strength had collapsed. He immediately ran towards Jijamata’s room. She was no more.

Shivaji Maharaj was deeply aggrieved with the demise of Jijamata. Yet he overcame the emotional turmoil knowing that he had the responsibility of running affairs of Swarajya in proper manner. Subsequently, he won the Fonda fort and constructed Sindhudurg and Vijaydurg sea forts. He formed a modern navy of the time to check on Portuguese, Dutch and English.

Shivaji Maharaj decided to expand his empire down south for which Kutubshah of Gowalkonda helped him. Shivaji Maharaj conquered the Jinji fort, Velur fort and some others.

Shivrai's stepbrother Vyankoji lived in southand Shivaji Maharaj wanted to involve himin the work of Swarajya; also he wanted to claim the share of half of the kingdom to which he was entitled after Shahjiraje. Maharaj asked Vyankoji to meet him and he explained him everything. However, he disagreed and sent his army to fight Shivaji. Shivaji's army defeated his army. He emerged victorious in Maharashtra.

Now Shivaji Maharaj was fifty years old. His health was failing. He was started bleeding. The doctors were treating him to their best yet it was of no use and ultimately on 3 April 1680, he succumbed to the illness. The first emperor of the Hindvi Swarajya left the world.

The nation lost one of the most brave, able devout warrior king. However, this colossal star of spirit and courage still continues to illuminate minds of people. The ideal of Magnum Opus of Swarajya, his attributes of humality, solidarity, froternity, exceptional administration skills, equility par excellence which go in making a great ruler continue to inspire us.